Distant

Voices

Canadian Politics

On The Outside Looking In

Michael B. Davie

Manor House Publishing Inc.

National Libary of Canada
Cataloguing in Publication Data

Davie, Michael B.

Distant Voices:

Canadian Politics on the Outside Looking In

Includes bibliographical references and notes.

ISBN 0-9685803-9-4

1. Political participation -- Canada. 2. Canadian
Alliance --Influence. 3. Opposition (Political Science)
--Canada. 4. Women in politics -- Canada. 5. Mass
media -- Canada -- Influence. 6. Mass media -- Political aspects -- Canda. 7. Canada -- Politics and government -- 20th Century.   I. Title.

JL65.D39 2001   324'.0971   C2001-903926-3

Published November 15, 2001
by Manor House Publishing: **(905) 648-2193**

First Edition.

Cover Design: Michael B. Davie.

By Michael B. Davie:

The Late Man MH
A Novel

Following The Great Spirit MH
Exploring Native Indian Belief Systems

Political Losers MH
The Lessons Of Failure

Distant Voices MH
Canadian Politics On the Outside Looking In

Canada Decentralized MH
Can Our Nation Survive?

Quebec and Section 33 MH
Why The Notwithstanding Clause Must Not Stand

Inside the Witches' Coven MH
Exploring Wiccan Rituals

Enterprise 2000 MH
Hamilton, Halton, Niagara Embrace the Millennium

Success Stories BR

Business Achievement in Greater Hamilton
Hamilton: It's Happening* BR
Celebrating Hamilton's Sesquicentennial

MH = Published by Manor House Publishing.
BR = BRaSH Publishing
* = With co-author Sherry Sleightholm

Belated Credit for Past Work:

Please note: Regarding the books Canada Decentralized, Quebec And Section 33 and Inside The Witches' Coven, all by Michael B. Davie, and Mystical Poetry by Deborah Morrison, Davie should have received credit for the cover design on all four books.

Regarding the book Enterprise 2000: Greater Hamilton, Halton and Niagara embrace the New Millennium, author Michael B. Davie should have received credit for the concept and design of the book's cover.

The cover depicted a limitless horizon with, in the foreground, a New Year's baby seated at a computer with the image repeated endlessly on the computer screen.

Davie also originated the back cover concept of the author leaning on the computer monitor showing the baby image, again repeated endlessly.

Photographer Paul Sparrow should have received credit for bringing these images to realization through his skilful photographic and computer montage work.

– Manor House Publishing Inc.

For
Philippa

Acknowledgements

This book would not have been possible without the thoughtful, analytical works of political scientists more seasoned and insightful than I.

I am grateful for the expert teachings of the political scientists I've cited in this book and for the patient distilling of knowledge by my McMaster University professors who helped me to earn honours degrees in Political Science.

As well, I appreciate the assistance extended by many conscientious people, too numerous to mention, in bringing this book to fruition.

My thanks, as always, to my wife Philippa for her constant encouragement and faith in the validity of my misadventures.

- Michael B. Davie.

About the author

One of Canada's most intriguing writers, Michael B. Davie is the author of such critically acclaimed business books as Enterprise 2000 and Success Stories.

The award-winning writer is also the author of nationally important books Political Losers, Canada Decentralized and Quebec & Section 33: Why the Notwithstanding Clause Must Not Stand. He also wrote The Late Man, his 10th book and first novel.

Michael B. Davie is also a journalist with The Toronto Star, Canada's largest newspaper, reaching millions of readers daily.

The author has won dozens of awards for outstanding journalism. His work has also appeared in such major Canadian newspapers as the Halifax Chronicle-Herald, Montreal Gazette, Calgary Herald, Winnipeg Free Press, Edmonton Journal and Vancouver Sun.

Prior to The Star, he was an editor with The Globe and Mail, Canada's national newspaper with coast-to-coast readership.

Previous to The Globe, he spent 17 years with The Hamilton Spectator, where he won 28 journalism awards.

Prior to joining The Spectator, he spent five years with other publications, including the daily Welland Tribune where he was a reporter, columnist and editor.

He also served two years as regional news

editor for one of Ontario's largest chains of community newspapers.

Born in Hamilton in 1954, Michael B. Davie's interest in writing began in early childhood. As a pre-school child, he became withdrawn and was in a state of shock after his parents decided to divorce. During a visit to a community centre, the child opened the door to a room to find child psychologists had been studying him through two-way mirrors.

The young child then began closely observing other children and adults, studying their interaction and watching their stories unfold. By the late 1960s and into the 1970s, while in his teens, he was a contributing writer to counter culture publications.

He turned professional in the mid-1970s as Editor of The Phoenix serving Mohawk College of Applied Arts & Technology where he earned a Broadcast Journalism diploma.

He also holds a Niagara College Print Journalism diploma and degrees in Political Science from McMaster University where he was repeatedly named to the Deans' Honour List and won the Political Science Prize for outstanding academic achievement.

Michael B. Davie currently resides in Ancaster with his wife Philippa and their children Donovan, Sarah and Ryan.

Contents

Manor House Publishing Inc.
(905) 648-2193.

Distant

Voices

Canadian Politics
On The Outside Looking In

Michael B. Davie

Manor House Publishing Inc.

Opening Notes

Distant voices.

Sometimes the words of women, the media and opposition parties strike a chord and make a difference in the political lifeblood of our country.

But more often than not, these political players are largely confined to the sidelines, on the outside looking in.

This book looks at these entities on the margins, examines why they're shunted to the sidelines and explores the circumstance by which they can and sometimes do play a more central role in shaping government policy.

Some readers may be surprised that I've included the media in this group of somewhat fringe political players. Surely the powerful media, credited with bringing down governments here and in the U.S., deserves a loftier status than that.

As a member of the media for nearly 30 years, as a reporter who has covered all levels of government, I can tell you that for the most part, the media often tries to influence the course of political events but frequently ends up merely reporting on the latest actions the government of the day has managed to get away with.

The biggest problem thwarting the media's influence is the public's rather short attention span.

We live in a world of hundreds of cable television channels and numerous major newspapers and radio stations.

And, of course, we also have the Internet with its universe of website publications and news and information sources.

In short, the public is swamped with an array of media competing for attention.

Making matters worse is the fact that most of us have relatively little time in our busy work days to pore over the issues of the day in sufficient detail. We also know that for the most part, there's little any of us can do to influence the government decision-makers.

But there are a couple of major exceptions to the scenarios I've just outlined:
Party leadership contests and elections.

For both events, the public and media express far more interest – and ultimately influence – than they often express for the day-to-day political goings-on.

It's during these times when politicians are held accountable and political reputations and futures are on the line that the media plays its most influential role.

At these events, a political misstatement or poor public speaking performance can quickly come back to haunt a politician in the form of lost support.

This book has a chapter dedicated to examining the role of the media during former Prime Minister Kim Campbell's successful bid for the PC leadership and her subsequent pounding at the polls during the following federal election.

There's also a chapter on the frustrating role of the Official Opposition party as performed by the Canadian Alliance Party.

In examining Alliance, we'll also take a look at how that party forms something of a continuum with its predecessors, Reform and Social Credit.

Although Alliance is definitely on the outside looking in, it's clear that this opposition party does, on occasion, wield some political influence.

While Alliance is usually not influential in terms of helping to shape government policy, the September 11, 2001 attack on the World Trade Center in New York pushed the party into a far more influential role.

Since the governing Liberals had no cohesive response to the attack, they simply stole Alliance's ideas – after first ridiculing them.

This, however, has proven to be a rare moment of importance for Alliance, a party that had, up until the terrorism attack, been confined to the sidelines.

While on the sidelines, Alliance had proven disorganized, embroiled in a leadership review and generally ineffective.

What a difference a day like Sept. 11 can make to a political party.

And there's the chapter on the participation of women in politics, which remains at fairly low levels.

Our chapter on women looks at what can be done to improve their participation in politics, noting that when you exclude the bulk of half your population from the decision-making procession, everyone loses.

In considering the reasons why these various groups on the outside looking in, you may begin to see ways in which their influence can be strengthened. In any event, our journey to the political fringe of influence begins now.

- **Michael B. Davie.**

Chapter One

Socreds, Reformers preceded today's Canadian Alliance

Today's Canadian Alliance party has a distant voice that is loudest in Western Canada.

It can also be heard more faintly from the Official Opposition benches at Parliament Hill in Ottawa.

Since the Canadian Alliance party has never formed a government, it is without question on the outside of power, looking in.

It will be noted, later in this chapter, that the party is not without influence at the federal level of government, although it plays no direct role in formulating policy.

However, this chapter will explore the history and dynamics driving this party, without dwelling too extensively on its tiresome leadership struggle that came to the forefront in the new millennium.

Canadian Alliance and its immediate predecessor, the Reform Party, bear some remarkable similarities to the Social Credit party which preceded both parties.

Indeed, this chapter will argue that both parties arose from like circumstances, and, fuelled by western Canadian alienation, can be viewed as a continuum of western unrest manifesting itself in political movements designed to appease westerners who feel left out a political process many believe is overly dominated by central Canada.

Based on extensive research, and by citing numerous sources, I'll draw several comparisons between both parties in regard to their economic policies and orientation, the role of Christian fundamentalist religion in both and the relationship of party leaders to their rank-and-file members.

Although differences exist between the two parties, the sheer strength of the similarities between them will serve to bolster this chapter's central argument that the two parties do indeed represent a continuum.

That the two parties should have originated in Alberta is not surprising.

The province's small population and isolation from urbanized Central Canada has fostered a feeling of being left out which in turn has resulted in the formation of protest movements intended to wrest a larger role for Alberta and the prairie provinces within the Canadian federation.

As Hugh G. Thorburn, head of political studies at Queen's University, observes:

> "The West has also been a nursery of protest movements The United Farmers or Progressive movement began the~ after 1918, as did the CCF-NDP and Social Credit in the 1930s."   1.

C. B. MacPherson notes the roots of western alienation can be traced back to confederatio.

This was a time when farmers in the prairie provinces began to view the National Policy as a development strategy favouring eastern business at the expense of the West, which many in this part of the country felt was being treated as something of a quasi-colonial economy.   2.

Bolstering MacPherson's argument, Chris Adams observes:
> "Since the establishment of Sir John A Macdonald's National Policy in 1879 which relegated the Prairie region to being an agricultural hinterland for the export of resources to Central Canada (Ontario and Quebec), the West has also been a seedbed of regional protest movements."   3.

Hard economic times can intensify a region's dissatisfaction with the existing power structure and increase the possibility of a protest party or movement achieving success.

It was just this set of conditions which prevailed when Social Credit became established during the Great Depression of the 'Dirty '30s'.

Alvin Finkle describes Social Credit, which ruled Alberta from 1935 to 1971, as a "depression-born movement for reform," which was "maintained in office by a wartime and post-war prosperity that allowed it to indeed achieve many reforms."   4.

The Reform Association of Canada formed in 1986, became the Reform Party of Canada in May 1987 and by the late 1980s through early 1990s, the fledgling party was attracting throngs of supporters from the West and from Ontario during the depths of a prolonged recession.

Although difficult economic times alone are insufficient to explain the popularity which has greeted Reform and the Socreds before them, such conditions can be seen as conducive to a protest party's efforts to attract support from a population which has grown disenchanted with the ability of mainstream parties to deal with economic woes.

A stronger common tie between Reformers and their forerunner Socreds is Western alienation.

As former Reform Party Leader Preston Manning explains in his own semi-autobiographical work, The New Canada, the common bond was the belief Reform's followers were being left out of the important political decision-making process:

> "The common issue that brought us together was a feeling of being left out of our own country. We left that the West's constitutional concerns were never given the same priority by the national government as those of Quebec... We believed that the solution lay not in mere protest or threats of separation, but in developing a short list of constructive changes, that is, reforms to the Canadian federal system and finding an appropriate political vehicle to promote that list (mainly) in the federal political arena."   5.

The West was a well spring for protest movements to empower the west. Manning recalls a boyhood steeped in populist culture:

"As I grew up, I learned that the 'prairie populism' with which I was familiar - the Social Credit movement in Alberta – was not an isolated political aberration, but 'part of a much broader political tradition. That tradition is as western as wheat, oil, forests, prairies, rivers and mountains."   6.

The tradition Manning speaks of extended throughout his own life, his father Ernest Manning's life and the life of the late Socred leader William Aberhart.

Aberhart, a radio preacher of evangelical Christianity, loosely based Social Credit on the same-named, radical monetary theory of British mechanical engineer Major Clifford Hugh Douglas who argued that although modern technology had made possible an age of prosperity for all, the concentration of wealth and power among elites had served to prevent a more even distribution of society benefits.

Douglas proposed monetary reforms to reduce the power of financial institutions he deeply distrusted. He also proposed a social credit or unearned dividend which individuals could then spend to raise production and consumption – and prosperity – across an entire society.   7.

Finkle suggests Aberhart little understood Douglas' complex theory but embraced with enthusiasm the disdain Douglas held for big business and big banks whom Aberhart label as "fifty big shots" who run Canada as an economic clique.

Aberhart also proposed, during his term, a social dividend which might have amounted to $25 per individual had it ever been implemented.

The Socred leader also attempted to limit the income of rich people to a set maximum.

He also wanted to have Alberta license banks and fix prices.   8.

However, the courts found Aberhart's Alberta government ultra vires – or guilty of acting outside provincial jurisdiction.
The court found the province was without the legal authority to regulate banks or alter federal monetary policies.

Although Aberhart continued to rail against big business and banks, he realized he could not assume control over them and he came to adopt a more conservative approach – including the appointment of conservative-minded officials to key boards developing financial policies that business found non-threatening.   9.

Similarly, when Aberhart died in 1943, his successor, Ernest Manning, introduced the Alberta Bill of Rights, which was also struck down as ultra vires by the courts as it too attempted to license and control banks under federal domain.

Manning then put monetary changes on hold and similarly took a more moderate stance. [10.]

Commenting on this necessary and practical tact, Finkle found pragmatism ruled the day and he summed up the Social Credit leader's approach thusly:

> "Unsurprisingly, the new Social Credit premier; Ernest Manning, forced to abandon the monetary panaceas of his party, simply concentrated on the provision of 'good government" ... it was not a radical right-wing regime and did not therefore represent a major shift from the earlier Aberhart regime." [11.]

Thus, when confronted with the legal limitations of their approach, both Social Credit leaders became less radical and more compatible with business.

Although Reform was not able to form a government, its leader Preston Manning succeeded in expanding the party's support in other areas of the country.

Manning achieved this success after he became more moderate after taking Reform from Western protest movement to national party with a more modest approach to broaden support.

For example, the Reform party's less radical approach favoured changing the GST rather than eliminating it.

Sydney Sharpe and Don Braid see a further influence of Social Credit on the Reform Party through the political bloodlines of the Mannings:

"The rightist Social Credit movement which ruled Alberta from 1935 to 1971 and elected many federal MPs provides the strategic goals, the grand design for Canada. Most of the ideas espoused by the Reform Party today, in fact, were developed by (Preston) Manning and his father in the late 1960s as they tried to keep the populist spirit alive in a form appealing to modern Canada." 12.

Religion is another common factor providing a continuous thread between Social Credit and Reform.

Offering his own expert commentary on Bible Bill Aberhart's ability to effectively mix religion and politics in a seamless web of social policy, John A. Irving quite astutely observes:

"Aberhart had no hesitation in presenting Social Credit to Albertans as a Divine Plan for the salvation of society, the parallel in the economic sphere of the Divine Plan for the individual. While such an approach infuriated many institutional religious and political leaders, it had a powerful attraction for thousands of people who were undoubtedly led in this way to join the movement." 13.

Murray Dobbin stresses the central role religion has played in Social Credit and Reform parties when he notes:

"Through Ernest Manning and his predecessor and mentor, William Aberhart, evangelical Christianity played a role in Alberta politics for which the only Canadian parallel is Catholicism in Quebec. Ernest Manning was both spiritual and political leader of Alberta. Preston Manning grew up in the shadow of his larger-than-life father." 14.

Preston Manning has made numerous appearances on his father's evangelical radio program 'Canada's National Bible Hour', was raised in a deeply-religious household and has served in an executive capacity on church boards.

In fact, Manning's church, the First Alliance (an ironic title given the party's subsequent mutation into Canadian Alliance) Church in Calgary, is a core part of the Christian and Missionary Alliance of Canada (again that word 'Alliance').

The First Alliance Church requires its members to accept the bible as true in every detail and to adopt all positions taken by the church. Commenting on 14 church articles on marriage, Dobbin says:

> "These articles of Preston Manning's faith are not simply his personal, private beliefs. They impel his actions and command him to act in the world to change it Preston Manning readily acknowledges the powerful influence of his faith on his thinking. The nature of that faith - its rejection of collectivism, its glorification of individualism and free enterprise, its view of women as submissive to men and homosexual men and women as the "basest of sinners," – must be reflected in "all spheres" of his life." 15.

Sharpe and Braide emphasize the importance of religion as a common bond between the Social Credit and Reform parties and as a shaper of Reform party policies when they assert that:

> "The deep religious convictions of the Manning family, rooted in evangelical Christianity, are central to Preston Manning's political beliefs.. He believes that every word of the Bible is true and knows he has a calling to translate these words into political action. Every one of his policies, from his views on capitalism to privatization, can be traced in a straight line back to his vision of the proper Christian society." 16.

Sharpe and Braid cite a number of examples in which Manning's religious beliefs have had an influence on party policy, much of which was drafted by Manning himself.

Examples include the party's code of conduct requiring Reform candidates to adhere to established Christian values.

And there was the party's very strong emphasis on individualism which manifested itself in opposition to multi-culturalism, bilingualism (except in very restricted governmental forms), special status for Quebec and any other measures which would put collective rights ahead of individual rights.

As Sharpe and Braid observe:
"Most Reformers firmly believe that the individual is paramount in society and that all group rights tend to infringe on individual rights. Preston Manning's own belief in individualism, in turn, springs from his deep religious convictions. If any one idea expresses the Reform Party's core ideology, it is this pure individualism with its strong echo of the western frontier." 17.

Sharpe and Braid further note that the late Social Credit leader 'Bible Bill' Aberhart, who "made little distinction between Alberta's secular and religious thrones," was succeeded as party leader by the equally religious Ernest Manning, while Manning's son, Preston Manning, "reached on such subjects as faith and politics..." 18.

Although Reform's agenda tended to magnify political reform over monetary changes, a close examination of both parties certainly indicates some important monetary policy similarities do exist to provide a common bond with the Social Credit party of the past.

Reform's Blue Book of policies supported the concept of a guaranteed annual income, a notion, which harkens back to Social Credit efforts to provide an unearned income, or social credit, to individuals to compensate for missing purchasing power.

As well, the Blue Book advocated studying some unusual concepts such as a negative income tax and a security investment fund, both of which could enhance the spending power of individuals in a manner Social Credit might well have supported. 19.

The Blue Book also called for privatization of Crown corporations, such as Petro Canada, in the belief – shared by Social Credit – that individual enterprise is by far preferable to control by a central, federal government.

Similarly, Reform also carried on with Social Credit's urging for voter recalls of ineffective elected members of government, increased use of referendums and decentralization of federal control over provincial resources.   20.

Although Reform did not seek to control banks and financial institutions in the way Social Credit had proposed, the Blue Book did call for the establishment of a greater number of regional banks to lessen the degree of concentrated financial power held by the Eastern banks.

Thus, while the proposed remedy differed, the perceived problem of indifferent Eastern banks remained the same.   21.

Reform also adopted Social Credit's distrust of federal government control over the resources of provinces.

In particular, Reform has lashed out against the former federal government of Pierre Trudeau for initiating the National Energy Program (NEP) which the party sees as a federal government theft of Western energy revenues.   22.

The Brian Mulroney government also came under fire by Reform for awarding a $1.4 billion CF-18 fighter plane contract to Montreal's Canadair Ltd.

This odorous decision came despite the technically and financially superior bid from Winnipeg's Bristol Aerospace.   23.

Faced with such perceived injustices, Preston Manning has advocated increased decentralization and devolution of powers from the federal government to the provincial governments.   24.

To Peter McCormick, Reform's concerns amounted to a milder version of the forces of frustration that aided in the creation of the Social Credit:

> "The current vituperation against federal bureaucrats and their left-leaning policy advisers is a weak reflection of the passionate hatred for the eastern banks and the sinister financial interests (the "Fifty Big Shots"), just as the GST is a poor substitute for the Depression that generated the second wave of populism in the form of the Social Credit and the CCF."   25.

Yet another similarity between Social Credit and Reform was the presence in both parties of a strong leader who played a central formative role in shaping party policy while giving the membership guidance and direction towards the carrying out of party objectives.

However, the extent of that direction has varied between leaders of both parties.

For example, the evidence suggests Aberhart ran Social Credit as something of a one-man show, which did not appear to take pains to reflect the wishes of rank-and-file members.

As MacPherson goes on to duly note:

"From the beginning, Aberhart's organization was strongly centralized... His headquarters, not a delegate convention, decided and announced that candidates would be run in every constituency, issued the draft platform and instructions to the constituencies, limited the agenda of the constituency conventions, and laid down the procedure for nominations. The central office took the initiative and kept control of the electoral machine." 26.

Although Finkle contends that the rank-and-file initially did have a voice and contributed to the process, he agrees with MacPherson that Aberhart did essentially hand-pick candidates and become more autocratic over time.

Finkle also stresses the importance of Aberhart's forceful, authoritarian leadership when he notes:

"No doubt Aberhart's demagogic style, used with equal effect to propound religious views and political views, was essential to the very rapid take-off of the Social Credit movement." 27.

Dobbin argues that Aberhart and Ernest Manning created the "illusion of democracy," often calling for "voice votes" on general goals in which an audience at a rally would roar approval of goals that had already been predetermined by the party leader.

It became very clear to political observers that both men doubted the ability of average citizens to make policy and so the two largely confined the citizens to serving as their cheerleaders or to filling other, lesser supportive roles.   28

Dobbin also suggests the steady shift towards a leader-dominated Social Credit party became even more pronounced under Ernest Manning:

> "By the time Ernest Manning took over the Social Credit League in 1943, it (the party) had already been transformed from a mass-based populist party and movement to a party electoral machine dominated by an increasingly autocratic leader and premier. Ernest Manning perpetuated that autocratic leadership and also moved the party further to the right."   29.

Sharpe and Braid have contended that the Reformers were headed in the same leader dominated direction as Social Credit:

> "Shrewd observers of Alberta Social Credit noted long ago that the Socred movement was not truly populist, but a massive delegation of trust by voters to revered leaders, first William Aberhart and then Ernest Man-

ning. The same dynamic appears at work today in Preston Manning's leadership of the Reform party. Audiences hang on his words with rapt attention, applauding every point and laughing at every joke."   30.

But Reform would not prove as autocratic as Social Credit.

Reform ran its conventions in a democratic manner, hearing the views and proposals of rank-and-file members and putting votes to ballots (although some "voice votes" were still conducted at rallies).

Reform also advocated voter recall rights and referendums, both of which would place more power in the hands of ordinary citizens – and not just during elections.

Yet there is no denying that Reform was also a leader-dominated party, a party in which leader Preston Manning took a comprehensive role in writing policies and advocating his own views while seeking audience approval of his statements.

Reform's philosophy, objectives and concerns had been given considerable thought and were largely formulated by the Mannings prior to the founding of Reform.

And, while the party insisted its directions are subject to input and amendments from ordinary members, Preston Manning played an enormous role in shaping policy.

Although the slight, owlish Manning lacked the forceful physical presence of either Socred leader discussed in this essay, it's also clear that he possessed different qualities which made him an effective leader.

Southam columnist Roy MacGregor suggested Manning's appeal may have laid in his unassuming, disarming manner.

In fact, MacGregor goes so far as to compare Manning with moviedom's stubborn and heroic little man who struggles against an indifferent government in Frank Capra's classic film 'Mr. Smith Goes to Washington'.   31.

Wherever the source of Manning's appeal lay, it's apparent that he was a strong leader and that Reform was certainly a leader-dominated party.

Although both of these characteristics may pale in comparison to those of Social Credit, these remain shared traits which mark a political continuum between the two parties.

By citing a number of political observers and political scientists, this chapter has drawn some important parallels between Social Credit and Reform and the Canadian Alliance parties, which, when taken together, demonstrate the existence of a political continuum.

We've found both these parties were born of Western alienation, nurtured by a profound distrust of the status quo and fed by a pronounced dislike and fear of powerful federal governments and Eastern business interests.

Both the Socreds and Reformers sought to wrest more power for the West by changing their provincial relationship with the federal government and by enhancing Alberta's financial strength.

For Social Credit, there were unsuccessful efforts to enact radical monetary reform and control of banks, while for Reform, the approach taken was largely one of advocating political reforms along with urging the establishment of additional regional banks, measures intended to enhance Alberta's political and financial clout.

Reform also looked favourably at some income enhancing measures in the spirit of Social Credit.

It is also true that Reform did not pursuing the radical bank-controlling measures once sought by Social Credit.

But this may have been for practical reasons since the illegality of such measures has made their pursuit a matter of sheer futility that even Social Credit came to abandon.

We've seen that with both parties, the response to the shared feeling of being largely "left out" of politics has been to form a new party offering solutions which, given their dramatic departure from existing power structures, can best be described as radical.

As well, we've explored the common bond of Christian fundamentalist religion as an integral part of both parties and a common tie linking Social Credit to Reform.

Finally, we've examined the existence of two leader-dominated parties led by what amounts to three generations of Christian fundamentalist leaders, from big 'Bible Bill' Aberhart to his protégé Ernest Manning (described by some as almost an adopted son of Aberhart who had only daughters), who lived for years at Aberhart's home, to Ernest Manning's own son, Preston, who has clearly inherited his father's strong appetite for religion and politics.

Given all of these remarkable similarities between the parties, and given Social Credit's evolution into an entity more comparable to today's Reform party, than Social Credit's origins would have suggested, one could view Reform as something of a 'Social Credit: The Next Generation'.

While that may be going a little too far, it's clear that the sheer number of similarities between the two parties amounts to a political continuum which has at its core the enduring legacy of Western discontent.

Although clearly on the outside, looking in, in terms of political power, the Alliance party has begun to play to a more central role in Canadian political life following the September 11, 2001 attack on the World Trade Center in New York.

Chantal Hebert, national affairs columnist for The Toronto Star, suggests Prime Minister Jean Chretien and the Liberal government are marching to the Alliance drummer when it comes to formulating policy in response to September 11.

Hebert notes that on Sept. 17, 2001, Alliance Leader Stockwell Day had repeatedly urged the Chretien government to "sign on to whatever military counteroffensive," the United States decided to engage in to fight against terrorism. Although the government roundly criticized Day for wanting to give the Americans a blank cheque, only days later, the government in fact committed troops with no questions aske, no clear objectives stated.   32.

The same day, the government rejected Day's call for tough anti-terrorism legislation, then a month later introduced an omnibus bill containing such legislation. As Hebert candidly observes: "Given the magnitude of Bill C-36, the ink was barely dry on Day's speech when the government set out to draft legislation." 33.

Hebert also notes that Day called for more resources for the military and an early budget – both of which were rebuffed and then quickly adopted by the government. 34.

Hebert adds: "Day may be the most discredited opposition leader in recent history, his party may sit in the basement of opinion polls, but that is not stopping the Chretien government marching to the war on terrorism to the Alliance drummer and much of the Canadian public from liking it." 35.

Indeed, although Alliance – like any opposition party – is a somewhat distant voice on the political landscape, that voice can indeed become louder and more influential in times of trouble when the government has no direction of its own to offer.

End Notes:

1. Hugh G. Thorburn, Party Politics in Canada, edited by Hugh G. Thorburn, (Scarborough: Prentice-Hall Canada , 1991), p. 317.

2. C. B. MacPherson, Democracy In Alberta: Social Credit and the Party System. (Toronto: University of Toronto Press, 1962), p.6.

3. Chris Adams, 'The Reform Party and the Roots of Western Protest' from Parliamentary Government. Vol.9. No. 1. Fall, 1989, p.14.

4. Alvin Finkle, The Social Credit Phenomenon in Alberta. (Toronto: University of Toronto Press, 1989) p1.

5. Preston Manning, The New Canada. (Toronto: Macmillan Canada 1992) p. V.

6. IBID, p.6.

7. Alvin Finkle, (Toronto: University of Toronto Press, 1989), pp. 33-35.

8. IBID.

9. C. B. MacPherson, Democracy In Alberta: Social Credit and the Party System. (Toronto: University of Toronto Press, I 962), pp. 177-178.

10. C. B. MacPherson, Democracy In Alberta: Social Credit and the Party System, (Toronto: University of Toronto Press, 1962), pp. 208-211.

11. Alvin Finkle, The Social Credit Phenomenon in Alberta, (Toronto: University of Toronto Press, 1989), p. 1.

12. Sydney Sharpe and Don Braid, Storming Babylon. Preston Manning and the Rise of the Reform Party. (Toronto: Key Porter Books, 1992), P. 7.

13. John A. Irving, The Social Credit Movement in Alberta. (Toronto: University of Toronto Press, 1974), p. 338.

14. Murray Dobbin, Preston Manning and the Reform Party. (Toronto: James Lorimer & Company, Publishers, 1991), p.1.

15. IBID, p. 11.

16. Sydney Sharpe and Don Braid, Storming Babylon. Preston Manning and the Rise of the Reform Party. (Toronto: Key Porter Books, 1992), p.2.

17. IBID, p. 172.

18. IBID, p. 82.

19. Principles And Policies: The Blue Book 1991, (Calgary: Reform Fund Canada, 1991), pp. 13-25.

20. IBID

21. IBID

22. Kenneth Whyte, Steve Weatherbe, Lori Cohen, Tim Gallagher and David Philip, 'The West Finds a Voice: A new federal party is launched', from Act of Faith: The illustrated Chronicle of the Reform Party of Canada. (Vancouver: B.C. Report Magazine Ltd., 1991), pp. 22-31.

23. IBID.

24. Mike Trickey, Southam News, 'Manning tells students beware of unity deal', Hamilton Spectator. September 29,1992. p. A1.

25. Peter McCormick, 'The Reform Party of Canada: New Beginning or Dead End?', from Party Politics in Canada. Edited by Hugh G. Thorburn, (Scarborough: Prentice-Hall Canada, 1991), p. 350.

26. C. B. MacPherson, Democracy in Alberta: Social Credit and the Party System. (Toronto: University of Toronto Press, 1962), p. 162.

27. Alvin Finkle, The Social Credit Phenomenon in Alberta. (Toronto: University of Toronto Press, i 989), pp. 30-41.

28. Murray Dobbin, Preston Manning and the Reform Party. (Toronto: James Lorimer & Company, Publishers, 1991), p. 16.

29. Murray Dobbin, Preston Manning and the Reform Party. (Toronto: James Lorimer & Company, Publishers, 1991), p. 17.

30. Sydney Sharpe and Don Braid, Storming Babylon. Preston Manning and the Rise of the Reform Party, (Toronto: Key Porter Books, 1992), p. 17.

31. Roy MacGregor, 'Preston Manning goes to Ottawa and talks common sense', The Hamilton Spectator. October 4, 1991. p. A6.

32. Chantal Hebert, 'Chretien marching to Alliance drummer', The Toronto Star, October 31, 2001. p. A29.

33. IBID

34. IBID

35. IBID.

Chapter 2

Women and Politics:
On the Outside Looking in

Although women comprise slightly more than half of the Canadian population, very few have reached the upper echelons of Canadian political life, fewer still command cabinet or senior civil servant positions, and, until the 1980s, not one had ever become the leader of a mainstream federal political party.

Women do indeed have distant voices on the political landscape. They are, with few exceptions, on the outside looking in.

As political scientist Janine Brodie has noted, despite the numerical strength of the female population; "within the rarefied atmosphere of our two major political parties, a 'women's candidate' remains a minority candidate."   1.

This chapter will cite and explore a number of obstacles that have hindered, and continue to hinder, political representation of women.

The slowly growing success of women in political parties, their historic difficulties, their remaining impoverished political position and their prospects for the future, all provide a framework for this chapter in which the area of study will largely be confined to the federal level of politics.

As well, statistical data will be examined to acquire an appreciation of the depth and breadth of the political under-representation of women.

Data will also be used to gain insight into the complexities associated with the concept of adequate representation of women's views at the federal level.

Based on the analysis and findings of numerous cited sources, I'll argue that women continue to be under-represented and still face obstacles towards achieving an enhanced level of representation, although significant gains are being made.

To that extent, this chapter will support the principal findings of a number of feminist writers whose work is appreciatively being relied on to advance this thesis.

However, within this central context, this chapter, on a secondary matter, will diverge somewhat from feminist thought to adopt my own, more-optimistic interpretation of data regarding representation as it relates to a slight gender gap.

I will argue that, based on data to be cited later in this chapter, the evidence suggests that on a number of issues, a majority of men and a majority of women share viewpoints.

Since some of these shared viewpoints are also reflected to some extent in the federal government's response to these issues, this in turn suggests that some views of women are achieving some degree of representation in parliament and that this is a measure of success that can be developed further.

Finally, after examining the causes of under-representation and inadequate participation rates of women at higher levels of office, this chapter will suggest measures which might have some success at removing lingering obstacles to help achieve greater participation and representation.

As early as 1883, Canada's first Prime Minister Sir John A. MacDonald introduced the first of three bills which would have resulted in legislation to enfranchise women. All three bills were defeated.   2.

It wasn't until 1916 that Alberta, Saskatchewan and Manitoba gave women the vote at the provincial level while British Columbia and Ontario followed suit a year later.

In 1917, the federal government then extended the franchise, but only to women who were British subjects, provided they were voting on behalf of a male relative in the armed forces.   3.

As Sylvia Bashevkin observed:
"Suffrage thus reached the national scene at the same time as women's contribution to the World War I effort was becoming increasingly evident, and when the Union government of Prime Minister Robert Borden faced a major electoral and political challenge concerning the issue of conscription."   4.

The federal government finally extended a full federal franchise to women in 1918.

But it would take another 11 years before the celebrated Persons Case would legally establish women as persons and make them thereby eligible to hold seats in the Senate.

As Brodie and Jill McCall Vickers note: "The campaign for the political emancipation of Canadian women took slightly more than half a century." 5.

If not for World War I, it's possible it may have taken even longer to dissolve the reluctance of otherwise-democratic nations to extend the franchise to women.

As Walter kohn observed:

"Women in Canada received the right to vote at the end of World War I. It was about that time that the franchise was extended to women in older democracies like Britain and the United States and in more recent ones like Germany and Austria. The war had brought about a recognition of the vital part played by women in the national struggle." 6.

Other 'democratic' nations were similarly slow to become full democracies.

Norway introduced women's suffrage in 1907 while France and Yugoslavia, recognizing the role women played in World War II, granted universal suffrage in 1945. 7.

Of course, suffrage wasn't so much 'granted' as won following the successful struggles of first wave feminists to obtain the vote.

While the wars indeed proved women capable of performing 'men's work' and taking on bill-paying and financial responsibilities usually then associated with men, as soon as wartime ended, there resumed a societal push in Canada and in other democratic nations to confine women to domestic life.

Commenting on France, Christine Faure suggested part of that push could be attributed to male insecurity:

"The more threatened the masculine population felt, the more they based their arguments on the sexual division of labour and social space defined in relation to the family. For them, the working-class woman's role was derived from a functional finalism; it was in her nature to be wife and mother, and thus not to work in the factory." 8.

Sharing an observation on the United States, Marianne Githens described a situation similar to Canada's when she noted the male-dominated societal push to confine women to traditional roles has a limiting result on political participation as "socialization to sex roles reduces the number of female candidates for public office." 9.

To further explain the inherent restrictions associated with what became the female gender role, Githens added:

"Socialization to the notion of the primacy of women's roles as mother and wife means that their involvement in other nontraditional female activity is contingent upon their first meeting traditional female role obligations. As a result, politically active women continuously face the strain or actual conflict of being above all else a wife and mother and simultaneously a full-time, dedicated, professional politician. In turn, the difficulty of meeting these dual demands dissuades women from participating in elite politics." 10.

This chapter is primarily concerned with Canadian women and is also largely confined to exploring participation at the federal level.

However, the preceding observations on difficulties women faced, and continue to face, in the U.S. and other large democratic nations, provide a set of useful reference points that relate to the Canadian experience.

For example, we can see that slowness in granting the franchise to women and the push to confine women to "traditional" activities were not peculiar to the largely hegemonic, male-dominated, socio-political entity of Canada but were instead part of a much wider experience.

This significantly amounted to an international set of female-oppressing values common to other English-speaking and French-speaking cultures which worked to legitimize the Canadian experience as one existing within wider North American and European trends.

This pervasive, intercontinental common denominator also served to dismiss as radical, those who would disagree with its commonly-held, though highly oppressive, assumptions about the place of women in society.

One set of assumptions centred around the concept of separate spheres: a public sphere in which men could practice politics and a private sphere, also dominated by men as head of the home, their 'castle'.

Although men were in charge of both spheres, women were supposed to take on a secondary role in the second, private sphere only.

The private sphere, in short, existed as the primary place for women.

As Sandra Burt observed:

"Life in Canada during the early part of the twentieth century was dominated by the belief that men and women lived in separate worlds. While a substantial number of women, particularly from the working class, were employed in a paid labour force, work was regarded as necessary for survival rather than a manifestation of women's rights. The male world was that of politics and paid labour. The female world was limited to household. The male clearly dominated the female world, and female's lives revolved around the activities of the men in their family. In this context, women's issues were restricted to what was considered relevant to family life, such as the education of children and the care of the home. There was a clear distinction between women's and men's issues." 11.

Yet as Burt also notes, the work force participation rate of women has grown substantially over the years.

While in 1901, women constituted only 16 per cent of the paid labour force, participation in the work force had climbed to 38 per cent by 1970.

Participation by women reached 50 per cent in 1980 – although participation was, and still is, concentrated somewhat heavily in low-paying clerical jobs. 12.

While women are participating in equal numbers in the work force, their role is often confined to the lower ranks of business organizations and little is being done by business or government to accommodate working women who are also carrying out the unpaid work associated with raising children and domestic life.

Regarding the struggle faced by female civil servants in particular, Nicole Morgan wrote:

> "They were trying to juggle their parental duties with full-time jobs. This was no longer 1965. when women of child-bearing age (between 25 and 39) accounted for only 28 per cent of all female public servants. In 1979, they constituted nearly 45.8 per cent of the female work force, a phenomenon never before seen in the labour market. These women were innovators in the career-and-family balancing act in a world that was (and still is) not ready to appreciate the art." 13.

To some extent, it would appear that the old separate spheres concept has not disappeared.

Instead, it has mutated into a variation of the original notion, with women now accepted as participants in both spheres, though generally at lower levels and with the proviso that work in the public world should be in addition to unpaid work in the private world.

I refer here to the 'superwomen' concept which arose in the popular media in the early 1980s: The unrealistic idea, if not outright expectation, that most women could do it all; raise a family, maintain a household and manage a successful career.

The necessary juggling act is a difficult undertaking laden with time constraints and the natural limitations associated with what essentially amounts to managing several jobs simultaneously.

Indeed, the burdens of domestic life and motherhood present formidable barriers which former British Prime Minister Margaret Thatcher, an occasionally-touted 'superwoman' did not have to face in her own successful career.

As Anna Coote and Polly Pattullo discovered of Thatcher:

"She has cheerfully admitted that she could not have combined a career with motherhood if she'd been unable to afford a 'first class nanny-housekeeper' and for that she relied on her husband's substantial income. Suppose she'd married not Denis Thatcher, company director, but Nigel Thatcher, struggling schoolmaster, or Basil Thatcher, underrated concert pianist? No nanny then. And no career... Margaret Thatcher's phenomenal success does not show that any woman (with ability, talent etc.) can become powerful in British politics. It demonstrates only what one particular woman can do in one particular – and by no means typical – set of circumstances." 14.

For those few women who do manage to enter politics, the experience can often be a frustrating enterprise that yields little to no added influence.

For example, there is a practice, common to both Canada and the U.S., of party elites steering women into 'lost cause' ridings that the party has little chance of winning.

This practice makes political sacrifices of women and ensures their political involvement is virtually meaningless.

Githens describes this practice, noting:

> "While political leaders have been anxious to secure women's volunteer and secretarial services, they have been hesitant to slate them as candidates. Or, when slated, they are sacrificial lambs with little chance of winning. And, once elected, they face a hostile reception from party leaders in their chambers."　　15.

Further insight into the phenomenon of women being used as sacrificial lambs in lost-cause ridings is provided by Brodie.

As Brodie notes, at the municipal level, where there is no clear hierarchy of gatekeepers and where there are fewer costs, women have found it easier to become successful candidates.

But at the federal level, entrenched hierarchies and old boys networks are very much in evidence.

As Brodie noted: "The success rates of women candidates in federal elections are still approximately one-half that of men."   16.

Arguing that women candidates are often deliberately guided in losing ridings and are not given the same opportunities for election as males, Brodie adds:

"Women candidates are less often elected, partly because they often choose to run for a minor party. More importantly, however, the major federal parties continue to follow the long-established tradition of nominating women to ridings where their chances of winning are low. Indeed, many of the representational gains that women have achieved over the past decade occurred precisely when their party was riot expected to win at the beginning of a campaign... Any optimism about the incvitability of women's representational gains should be tempered with a hard dose of political reality. Nominating women to seemingly lost-cause ridings and waiting for electoral volatility and an unexpected electoral tide to sweep them into office is hardly a promising strategy for increasing the political representation of women in Canada."   17.

Brodie also notes the heady cost of contesting any party nomination has risen considerably over the past decade, and now presents a significant barrier to women due to the widespread phenomena of women.

These women are often marginalized in lower income jobs and due to their more limited access to financial resources, they have a tougher go to gain acceptance.

As Brodie observes:
"Women may be more prepared to offer themselves as candidates for public office than in the past, but unless controlled, financial constraints will increasingly and effectively far them from effective competition in the future. Increases in campaign expenditures threaten the political gains in political representation of all groups that sit disproportionately at the bottom of the socio-economic hierarchy." 18.

Indeed, added to ongoing barriers of societal attitudes, unreasonable expectations, low incomes and discrimination encountered by women experiencing the informal politics of the workplace, are the same barriers facing women in formalized politics.

Bashevkin's compelling study of women's participation in major party organizations discovered a phenomenon she described as "the higher the pay, the fewer at play": the higher one looked into the upper echelons of major parties, the fewer women there were to be found.

Bashevkin then concluded "higher, more powerful and more competitive positions throughout English Canada remain overwhelmingly in the hands of men." 19.

Bashevkin found that party women generally held 'pink collar', largely clerical or office support positions.

Where women did occupy the upper rungs of a party organization, it was generally in lost-cause ridings where organizers were expected to perform something of a caretaker function.

This phenomenon Bashevkin termed "the more competitive the fewer": The more competitive a riding, the fewer the women occupying upper echelon positions. 20.

Chantal Maille noted all three major federal parties have created special funds to support women candidates.

But Maille also notes that "the sums allocated are very minimal in comparison with the expenditures anticipated." 21.

Maille also found women well represented in lower and middle party ranks but nearly absent in upper ranks.

She cited a number of reasons for this:
"The higher the rank, the fewer the women, and this can be attributed to several factors: socialization, unequal responsibility for housework and childrearing, failure to conform to the socio-economic model favoured by the political parties, weak networks within the parties, and the exclusion of informal power networks from the structure." 22.

Not that there haven't been strides. For example, during the 1988 federal election, women comprised a record 19.2 per cent of candidates and a record 1.75 per cent of elected members.

However, Maille adds a sobering thought when she points out that at the current growth rate, and not allowing for setbacks, which would likely occur, "it will take nine elections, or nearly 45 years until an equal number of women and men are elected to the House of Commons." 23.

I am arguing that barriers against women should be removed and that there should be substantially more women in elected and appointed positions to reflect their numerical strength.

But I am not arguing for a strict numerical equality of male and female elected representatives, as quota systems can often go awry and result in clearly unacceptable degrees of reverse discrimination.

In short, quota systems siumply don't work.

The goal, in my view, should be to remove barriers and fairly open up the electoral process to make it more likely that the best person – regardless of gender – earns office. This would undoubtedly result in far more women being elected.

If the political playing field can truly be made level, this could result in more women than men in some parliaments, and less women than men in others.

Underlying this argument is my belief that on many issues, the thinking of most women is not substantially different than most men.

To support this argument, I will refer to the 1988 Canadian National Election Study which found only generally slight gender gaps between the opinions of men and women on a number of issues.

In contrast, the study illustrated more significant gaps existed between the views of most women and the views of feminist women, with still wider gaps between views of most men and those of feminist women.   24.

When the study asked participants if they agreed abortion should be a personal choice, most women (51.3 per cent) did not agree, while 48.7 per cent agreed.

Results were somewhat similar for men, with most (54.4 per cent) not agreeing, and a minority (45.6 per cent) agreeing.

For feminist women, the results were the other way around with most (55.6 per cent) agreeing and a minority (44.4 per cent) not agreeing.

Although the margins are not enormous, the results do show that while most feminist participants see abortion as a matter of personal choice, this view is not shared by most women in general or by most men. 25.

To cite another example: A majority of all three groups did not agree that the government should fund daycare centres but the issue came close to splitting feminists down the middle with 48.9 per cent agreeing and 51.1 per cent not agreeing.

In contrast, wider margins of women and men did not agree with funding while 44.3 per cent and 37.8 per cent respectively, agreed.   26.

On still other questions: A majority in all three groups opposed nuclear submarines although the level of opposition was highest from feminists (69.3 per cent) followed by women (67.5 per cent) and men (56.1 per cent).

A majority in all three groups also agreed the government should do more to help single parents, the elderly, the poor and small business, although in each case, feminists registered the strongest degree of overall support and men the lowest amount of support in this survey.

Although a majority of women and men did not feel the government should do more to help women, a modest majority of feminists (55.1 per cent) felt the government should do more.   27.

Perhaps some of the majority viewpoints have had an influence on the federal government which has not left abortion as a matter of private choice, has cancelled its expensive nuclear submarine program and is not funding day care.

If so, this amounts to a very mild, if somewhat positive sign, that the government is listening to the people it represents.

The government, also like the study participants, is divided on other issues, and most people undoubtedly look for more than divided opinions from government.

While mainstream views of women may be somewhat reflected in government, feminists views tend to be further left of centre.

As Brodie observed:
"Feminist women, however, differ significantly from other women on a broader range of issue positions. They are, for example, much more likely to advocate reproductive choice, government funding for daycare and increased government support for all the subgroups listed. As in other countries, feminist women appear to occupy a place on the political s spectrum that is further to the left than that occupied either by men or women who indicate that they have not been positively influenced by the women's movement."   28.

Although feminist views are often outside of the mainstream of accepted political norms, that does not mean they are not worth pursuing.

I would argue that the feminists' stronger emphasis on day care subsidization, additional support for single parents, and added support for women in general, are all in the best interests of women even though these issues have drawn less support from the wider female population.

Day care and single-parent-support both go to the heart of freeing women from biological-domestic constraints, putting them in a better position to provide their children with a caregiver while they then pursue employment.

This in turn could provide these women with a degree of experience, income and participation that might then help them to promote themselves or achieve public office or an enhanced role within a political party.

Financing such measures may be troublesome given the federal government's $400-billion debt and its average $30-billion deficit (in the 1990s) which annually adds to a debt load already consuming almost half of every tax dollar to interest payments.

Yet, the benefit of having greater numbers of women fulfill their potential makes the possibility of a greater role for the government worth examining further.

In addition to some form of enhanced day care and single parent assistance, the participation of women can also be increased through modifications to our education system to better promote gender equality and foster a better understanding of the need for increased female representation.

Efforts also need to be made through the media, including advertising, and through families to break free of gender stereotyping.

Females, and males, are still subjected to hegemonic societal values which are then internalized with the end result of limited potential and horizons for both genders.

Dr. Margaret Matlin has noted that prejudicial forms of socialization begin virtually at birth with infants immediately slotted into pink, passive girls or blue, energetic boys.

Citing a number of clinical studies observing the reaction of adults to a baby (some were told it was male, others were told it was female) Dr. Matlin noted the results demonstrated that preconceptions still serve to narrowly define, and thereby limit, people in terms of unwarranted sets of expectations.   29.

As Lise Gotell and Brodie have warned, there still exists a societal tendency to treat women's issues as private rather than public issues, marginalizing matters of importance and splitting women along class, family, religious and ethnic lines.   30.

As well, Linda Kealey and Joan Sangster warn of right-wing nationalist movements hostile to feminism and eager to again con fine women to the private sphere and traditional roles.   31.

The approach to deal with problems of perception and misunderstandings associated with the political potential of women may lie with forging alliances with the greater female and male populations.

While gender gaps exist, it is also encouraging to note that in many cases the gap comes down to a matter of which gender group majority supports a given measure to the greatest degree.

Support itself is not at issue, only the size of the male and female majorities behind it. This of course, is the crux of the issue.

As indicated earlier, mainstream political messages from women may finally be getting through to government.

The task now may be to convince more women to accept that such feminist concerns as day care and support for single parents (almost invariably women) are issues which women everywhere should support.

The sense of fair play held by many men might also be utilized to build a wide majority of support for such measures to an extent that the federal government will find it difficult to dismiss them as private 'women's issues'.

As well, parties should be pressured into setting reasonable spending limits on nomination contests and adopting rules which encourage the inclusion of women while putting an end to the possibility of dirty tricks or backroom deals thwarting a woman's chance of electoral success.

And, government and business should practice the fair promotion of women and legislation may be needed to open up sources of accessible financing for women going into politics or business.

All of these measures, if adopted, would go a long way towards addressing some of the long-standing inequities and unfair qualities associated with the representation and political participation of women.

More than anything else, however, a societal shift in attitude is required: There needs to develop a common understanding that beyond the human costs borne by women, our society as a whole is the poorer for having held back women.

We are poorer for having prevented half our nation's population from realizing its full potential, for having squandered the fuller contribution that might have been, and for having failed to open the door to new ideas and new approaches.

Until these issues are fully addressed, women in general will continue to be a distant voice on the political landscape.

END NOTES:
For Chapter Two

1. Janine Brodie, "The Gender Factor and National Leadership Conventions in Canada," from Party Democracy in Canada (Toronto: Prentice Hall, 1988) p.187.

2. Status of Women Canada, Federal Government of Canada, Towards Equality For Women. (Minister of Supply and Services Canada, 1979), p. 3.

3. IBID, p. 4.

4. Sylvia Bashevkin, Toeing the Lines; Women and Party Politics in English Canada, (Toronto: University of Toronto Press, 1985) p.10.

5. M. Janine Brodie and Jill McCalla Vickers, 'Canadian Women in Politics: An Overview,' The Politics of the Second Electorate, (Ottawa, 1982), pp. 1-5.

6. Walter S. G. Kohn, 'Women in the Canadian House of Commons,' American Review of Canadian Studies 1984, 3, 1984, p. 298.

7. Maurice Duverger, The Political Role of Women, (United Nations Commission on the Status of Women/Unesco, Paris: 1953), p. 13.

8. Christine Faure, Democracy Without Women, (Indianapolis, Ind.: Indiana University Press, 1985), p. 3.

9. Marianne Githens, Political Women. Edited by Janet A. Flammang, (London: Sage, 1984), p. 46.

10. IBID pp. 47-48.

11. Sandra Burt, 'Women's issues and the Women's Movement in Canada since 1970,' from The Politics of Gender, Ethnicity and Language in Canada. Edited by Alan Cairns and Cynthia Williams, (Toronto; University of Toronto Press, 1986), p. 112.

12. IBID pp. 117-119.

13. Nicole Morgan, The Equality Game. Women in the Federal Public Service (1908-1987). (Ottawa: Canadian Advisory Council on the Status of Women, 1988), pp. 43-45.

14. Anna Coote and Polly Pattullo, Power and Prejudice. Women and Politics (London: Weidenfeld and Nicholson, 1990) p.7.

15. Marianne Githens, Political Women. Edited by Janet A. Flammang, (London: Sage Publications Inc., 1984), p. 15.

16. Janine Brodie, 'Women and the Electoral Process in Canada,' from Women in Canadian Politics: Toward Equity in Representation. (Toronto: Dundurn Press, 1992), Pg. 11.

17. IBID.

18. IBID. pp. 5-6.

19. Sylvia Bashevkin, Toeing the Lines: Women and Party Politics in English Canada, (Toronto: University of Toronto Press, 1985), p. 79.

20. IBID.

21. Chantal Maille, "Primed for Power: Women in Canadian Politics," Background Paper for Canadian Advisory Council on Status of Women, November 1990. p. 23.

22. IBID.

23. IBID, p.10.

24. Canadian National Election Study as presented in "Women and the Electoral Process in Canada," by Janine Brodie, from Women in Canadian Politics: Toward Equity in Representation. Toronto: Dundurn Press, 1992. pp. 20-21.

25. IBID.

26. IBID.

27. IBID.

28. Janine Brodie, "Women and the Electoral Process in Canada," from Women in Canadian Politics: Toward Equity in Representation, Toronto: Dundurn Press, 1992. p. 22.

29. Margaret W. Matlin, The Psychology of Women, (Toronto: Holt, Rinehart and Winston Inc., 1987) pp. 7-14.

30. Lise Gotell and Janine Brodie, 'Women and Politics: More than an issue of Numbers,' from Party Politics in Canada, edited Hugh G. Thorburn. Scarborough: Prentice-Hall of Canada 1991), pp. 58-61.

31. Linda Kealy and Joan Sangster, Beyond the Vote. Canadian Women and Politics, Toronto: University of Toronto Press, 1989), p. 8.

"...experience as a writer shows... (How The Messengers Shape The Race) is very well written... combines good writing skills with good research."

- Andre Turcotte
Political Science Professor,
McMaster University,
 May 1993.

Chapter 3

How the Messengers
Shape The Race

The Role of Media and Polls
in The PC Leadership Contest

The media can be considered a distant voice in
Canadian politics – most of the time.

The media isn't privy to cabinet meetings and
doesn't establish policies. Even when it reports on
political incompetence or wrongdoing in government,
there are often few direct results.

The few exceptions include elections and party leadership contests. During these events, the response to an embarrassing story can be immediate.

To see how the media had relatively little impact on a leadership race, but a larger impact on the subsequent election, I'll revisit an historical footnote: Kim Campbell, one of Canada's shortest serving prime ministers.

Did we see the 'coronation' of Kim Campbell?

No, Campbell's victory in gaining the federal Progressive Conservative leadership crown did not come without effort.

This victory was earned, not granted.

The 1993 party leadership race to replace Brian Mulroney as leader quickly became the subject of a struggle, a true contest made more competitive by the influential presence of the media.

This chapter will examine the role of the media in shaping the leadership race through its long-standing practices of focusing on the leading candidate's shortcomings, enlarging the profile of the strongest rival candidate, determining what many of the issues are, and, to a large extent, helping to set the political agenda.

We'll also explore the way delegate opinion polls help shape the race by giving one candidate, Campbell, the image of an early winner, thereby convincing potentially strong candidates to not take part in the race while she draws added support based on a 'winability' factor.

Drawing on a wealth of sources, from public opinion polls to analytical newspaper and magazine articles, to my own observations as a seasoned journalist, this paper will argue that the messengers – the media and the polls – play key roles in shaping the race, including depicting the contest as something of a horse race, agenda-setting, helping establish who the main contenders are from a field of candidates, while also determining what some of the issues are.

I'll also show that the media, by employing a broader degree of public scrutiny of the leading candidate, helps to ensure that the leadership contest is made far more competitive.

Within weeks of Prime Minister Brian Mulroney's February 24, 1993 resignation announcement, PC cabinet minister Kim Campbell became a very strong front-runner for the position of party leader (and with it, PM) before she even declared her candidacy.

A Mclean's magazine-COMPAS survey conducted March 1-4, 1993, and based on a random sampling of 450 of the 3,293 delegates who attended the 1991 PC national convention, showed 38 per cent of those polled favoured Campbell as their first choice to succeed Mulroney.   1.

The poll showed senior cabinet ministers Don Mazankowski and Michael Wilson lagged way behind in the approval ratings, with 8 per cent and 7 per cent respectively.

Former Prime Minister Joe Clark was tied with cabinet newcomer Jean Charest with just 5 per cent, cabinet minister Perrin Beaty received 4 per cent, and MPs Garth Turner and James Edwards were tied for last with a paltry 1 per cent each.   2.

Campbell was also ranked highest when the same poll asked participants who is most capable of beating the Reform party and who is most capable of beating the Bloc Quebecois. She also scored above the others as one who exercises good judgement.   3.

The margin of popularity for Campbell, as indicated by the poll, indicated she could win on the first ballot if the convention had been held in early March.

It also showed that if it went to a second ballot, she would humiliate her nearest rival by capturing a crushing victory with 68 per cent of the vote. 4.

As Mclean's writer Anthony Wilson-Smith notes, the affect of Campbell's enormous early lead – and its inherent promise of an embarrassing defeat to any opponents – was enough to dissuade Trade minister Michael Wilson and other prominent cabinet ministers to declare they would not be entering the race.

As Wilson-Smith adds:
"Among other contenders, the first casualty of Campbell's strength was Wilson, initially considered a certain candidate."   5.

The prominent coverage given the findings of the poll by Canada's national news magazine and by other media succeeded in magnifying Campbell's image as a potentially strong winner.

This was a decided advantage for attracting funding in a contest where the cost of running can approach $1-million.

Such a well-publicized gap between the front-runner and other potential opponents makes any contenders look like 'also-rans' before they even declare their candidacy.

The long-shot status of other potential candidates can make it difficult for them to raise campaign funds and some choose instead to follow the leader.

As Anthony Wilson-Smith notes:

"One day after the poll was released, Communications Minister Perrin Beatty, who had been considered a certain candidate, announced that he would not run and threw his support behind Campbell.... Worried that he might be embarrassed by a poor showing, Charest also came close to backing out. He met with Mulroney privately the day before his announcement and solicited advice from close friends and supporters, many of whom had divided emotions and opinions because they questioned his ability to raise enough money to run a credible campaign."   6.

The effect of public opinion polls in magnifying the front-runner's advantage has also been explored by political scientist Roger Gibbons.

Commenting on this phenomenon as it applied to the 1984 federal election, Gibbons observed:

"The 1984 polls, which from early in the campaign indicated a Conservative landslide, arguably had at least three important although not necessarily decisive effects. First, they undercut morale within the Liberal campaign organization, making it difficult to attract financial support and volunteer assistance. Second, they undercut the Liberal campaign strategy in the West; Western Canada wanted an effective voice in Ottawa, there was little sense in voting for the Liberals as the Conservatives were expected to win. Third, they assured Quebec voters that a shift to the PC party would not isolate Quebec from the federal government." 7.

Yet, the intense media exposure given a strong front-runner can also be something of a double-edged sword that can cut against the leader by making her a target for the kind of close scrutiny her opponents are largely spared.

As COMPAS president and Carleton University Political Science Professor Conrad Winn points out, Campbell's big lead "could paradoxically do her harm by enticing journalists and politicians to make her 'work for her money." 8.

Indeed, there is substantial evidence to suggest the media did in fact make Campbell work for her money: Even an otherwise soft feature article in Mclean 's carried several harmful observations, including Campbell's tendencies to exaggerate academic credentials and proficiency at languages and her at-times abrasive personality.

Mclean's writers E. Kaye Fulton and Mary Janigan found her to be brash, disdainful of others' views and resentful of criticism. 9.

News reports of Mike Wilson's belated endorsement of Campbell also carried Liberal deputy leader Sheila Copps' criticism that the move shows that the two are "the king and queen of the GST," suggesting Campbell was closely tied to unpopular Tory policies.   10.

A May 11 story carried in The Hamilton Spectator noted that Campbell was then well ahead in the race with 1,130 committed delegates versus 600 for Charest and 707 undecided.

But the story also noted it was unclear whether Wilson's move will give Campbell's campaign "added momentum or weigh it down with unwanted baggage."   11.

The Spectator also carried a report suggesting that Campbell was becoming overconfident about winning and drew attention to her remark – seen as arrogant by some political observers – that it would be better for the party if she was elected leader on the first ballot.   12.

In marked contrast to earlier print and electronic media coverage praising her intellect and drive, Campbell spent much of mid-May fending off reports in Mclean's and in newspapers across Canada which suggested she was very much a part of the arrogant old guard of the party.

Then, the front-runner put her foot in her mouth during the May 14 leadership debate with her remark denouncing as "enemies of Canada," those disagree with the GST and Tory efforts to fight the deficit. She apologized the following day.   13.

The media's task of exposing Campbell's weaknesses and gaffes was made easier by Jean Charest's organizers who circulated a two-week-old Vancouver magazine article in which Campbell had made a number of politically foolish, candid remarks.

These remarks included her assertion that people who complain about government while being proudly apathetic are "condescending SOBs," her comment that Joe Clark won a prior leadership contest because he was the "least hated" of the contenders and her reference to "evil demons of the papacy."   14.

Victoria-based government affairs consultant Paul Nicholson told John Geddes of The Financial Post that the furore over Campbell's remarks in Vancouver magazine breathed new life into the arrogant image she had in her past with British Columbia's Social Credit government.

He added that Campbell's initial positive publicity may have created its own backlash.   15.

The Toronto Star noted that Campbell refused to apologize for her remarks and insisted, that in their fuller context in Vancouver magazine, they were inoffensive. It was a poor response to a major issue.

And The Star also noted that the Canadian Conference of Catholic Bishops did find the remarks offensive.   16.

Carol Goar, The Star's national affairs columnist, said Campbell's ill-advised, arrogant-appearing remarks show she is "not a fully formed politician," in contrast to Charest whom Goar described as "a surprisingly well-rounded politician," who has shown he can "talk intelligently about economic policy, federal-provincial relations, social reform, education, and, of course, Quebec."   17.

Peter O'Neil, Ottawa correspondent for The Vancouver Sun, said Campbell's remarks reveal her conceit, arrogance, mean streak and dismissive attitude to others.   18.

As if this dark assessment of Campbell's personality wasn't damaging enough, O'Neil challenged her linguistic and economic credentials with this quote from Peter C. Newman:

> "She has never held an economic portfolio and seems uninterested in this vital aspect of her mandate; her French is not as fluent as advertised, most dangerous of all, she has roused expectations that no politician can satisfy."   19.

You might expect the media's intense scrutiny of Campbell, particularly on matters concerning her proficiency with the French language and her attitude toward the Roman Catholic religion, to have had an impact on getting members of the public to take a more critical look at the woman who would be prime minister. This certainly appears to be the case.

While Campbell was busily defending herself from media attacks, a poll in Quebec suggested her rival Jean Charest had a higher level of support from voters in Quebec and would surely fare better than Campbell, the Bloc Quebecois and the Liberals in capturing the votes of Quebecers, a finding that Charest quickly interpreted as evidence he would be more capable of keeping the PCs in government. [20].

Another poll, by Angus Reid, of a broader cross section of the Canadian public suggested that if Charest became party leader, he could lead the Tories to victory in a federal election, while if Campbell led the Tories, the Liberals would win. [21].

It is important to note that both polls concerned the general public. PC delegates differ from the public in their strong support of Tory policies such as free trade. [22].

We should also note that Campbell had almost twice as many committed delegates as Charest, though not enough to win a first-ballot victory.

However, I would suggest that the cumulative, influential impact of media scrutiny of Campbell, and the release of results from the recent polls, combined to undermine a previously foregone conclusion that Campbell would be the clear winner.

With her 'federal election winability' in question, Campbell faced the possibility, the risk, that some of her Quebec delegates would have perceived that they are no longer backing a 'winner' and would regroup to back Charest, following a long-standing tradition of backing a potential winner who is also a native son of Quebec.

Charest could also succeed in capturing more of the uncommitted delegates while Campbell could lose some of her 'soft support' delegates – and not just from Quebec – who uneasily backed her, more because they thought she would win rather than out of any deep-seated conviction that she would make the best leader.

As The Spectator's former Ottawa Bureau Chief John Flanders noted in 1993, a quarter of 3,846 delegates were uncommitted and, he noted, "those uncommitted delegates are important because leadership front-runner Kim Campbell is still hundreds of votes short of a first-ballot win to become prime minister." 23.

Opinion polls and media reporting of the event carried the combined impact of directly influencing the cut and thrust of an intensifying campaign.

As widely-respected political journalist Jeffrey Simpson observed:

"Polling numbers take on a life of their own; and perception becomes reality. Once the media rush to judgement following a given poll or series of polls, the politicians instinctively feel they must shift their behaviour accordingly."   24.

In Campbell's case, her response to the onslaught of recent polls and media criticism has been to shift her campaign from one of simply promoting her leadership abilities, to one that was quire defensive in character.

She later took to apologizing for some remarks, defending others and stating defensively that she still had her committed delegates on side despite the polls.   25.

The leadership campaign's focus had also shifted from its former low-key preoccupation with a mix of issues and leadership qualifications, to one in which the overwhelming emphasis is on the simple question of who will win the race.

Aided by the opinion polls, the media helped

transform a coronation into more of a horse race.

Commenting of the impact of media reporting of polls, Simpson observed:

> "Whether they are accurate or not, misleading or otherwise, the polls are the yardstick by which too many journalists measure political success. And this in turn, contributes to the horse-race kind of reporting that so colours elections and what transpires between them." 26.

As a journalist with more than 25 years experience, I've observed that accuracy and fairness can indeed take a back seat to the overriding desire of the media to use polls as a means of shaping a race.

A race is more exciting and far more newsworthy than a coronation.

The mere fact that the media collectively wants a race and will try to create one is often enough to ensure there is one.

Having previously covered a number of federal and provincial elections, I can also attest to the tendency of the media to create a more competitive race.

The media does this by playing up polls that go against the front-runner who is also subjected to a level of scrutiny her opponents are largely spared.

As a journalist with The Welland Tribune in the late 1970s, my own interviews with Tory Leader and former Prime Minister Joe Clark told me that he was a leader of far greater substance than was indicated by a barrage of stories ridiculing him for his appearance or for losing luggage.

During the 1980s, as a journalist with The Hamilton Spectator, I covered the collapse of Ontario's Tory dynasty and was appalled by the way PC Leader Frank Miller was constantly portrayed by other media as a small-town huckster and former used car salesman in loud jackets.

The jackets were certainly loud but Miller's experience as a used car salesman in Bracebridge, in northern Ontario, was confined to a summer job in his youth.

In contrast, Miller's extensive university education and political credentials were given short shrift as the media created, and then perpetuated, his rube image.

As Clive Cocking has observed:
"The normal journalistic reaction is not to praise but to criticize... Criticisms, charges and accusations produce the most jolts on television news and the biggest headlines in newspapers." 27.

Indeed, the media has surpassed political parties when it come to either shaping a candidate's persona and image or when it comes to finding and reporting damaging information on a candidate.   28.

Initially, as in the case of Campbell, image-shaping by the media can work to the advantage of a new, front-runner candidate, by generating a huge amount of largely favourable, image-building publicity.

Reflecting on this phenomenon as it applied to Pierre Elliot Trudeau during his leadership race, Christina McCall-Newman recalled:

> "Long after his victory, Trudeau's opponents, notably the supporters of John Turner and Paul Hellyer, continued to feel the presentation of him as a reluctant leader was sheer image-making, claiming that his leadership campaign was brilliantly plotted to attract press attention without appearing to do so, contrived to look uncontrived, right down to the last wet-eyed, short-skirted Trudeau hostess in the crowds at the convention hall."   29.

Fred J. Fletcher and Daphne Gottlieb Taras cite two more well-known cases of the media making – and breaking – political images when they observe:

> "Liberal Leader John Turner is a good example of a politician who was initially glorified by the media, becoming something of

a political legend while he was out of public life (and the glare of media scrutiny), but whose weaknesses – probing stare, nervous cough, and brittle delivery – were magnified by television. It seems that his "image problem" was a major factor in his two electoral defeats. Former PC Leader Joe Clark was also victimized by a media that would not tolerate a non-telegenic leader." 30.

Beyond making and breaking images, the media helps set the political agenda.

Referring to this "important role of agenda-setting," Mark Dickerson and Thomas Flanagan explain:

"Attention is a scarce resource; people cannot think about everything at once. The media do not tell people what to think, but they may tell people what to think about. And this is of the highest importance in politics because interest groups, parties and ideologists often differ profoundly in their assessment of what constitutes a problem worth thinking about." 31.

Commenting further on the media's ability to set the political agenda, political scientists Robert Hackett and Lynne Hissey observe:

"Such influence can be seen in two ways. First, by directing audience attention towards some aspects of reality and away from others, the news media help define reality for their audiences and to structure the public's perception of the political world. Contrary to popular belief news does not simply 'reflect' reality: the mere necessity of selecting some events to cover while ignoring others, and choosing language and frameworks in which to describe these events, makes such a goal impossible."   32.

A good example of media agenda-setting in the Tory leadership race was the marijuana-smoking issue which clearly was a matter none of the candidates would have wanted to make an issue on their own.

Charest and Campbell both admitted they'd smoked up in their youth but Campbell once again put her political foot in her mouth when responding to a follow-up question.

When asked why, as a former justice minister, she didn't liberalize marijuana laws given that she herself had broken the law by smoking marijuana, Campbell stupidly replied that holding marijuana in her hand and smoking it did not mean that she was in possession and so she therefore had not broken any law.

This assertion drew a belly laugh from prominent lawyer Clayton Ruby who wondered aloud on CBC television why Campbell, a lawyer, was apparently unaware that smoking marijuana is illegal and that holding it in your hand is of course considered possession, as anyone arrested with a 'joint' in their hand can attest.   33.

The marijuana smoking issue was kept on the public agenda for several days in May, as Campbell repeated her bizarre possession statement to reporters, and added that she does not favour easing possession penalties.

She then made matters considerably worse when she angrily stated that she she was sorry she did not lie when she was asked if she had smoked it.   34.

Through all of this, Charest had been a net beneficiary. while Campbell had been forced to defend herself on an array of issues already discussed in this chapter, Charest had undergone far less intense scrutiny.

He was presented instead as the main rival, the one contender who could wrest the Tory crown from Campbell before it is ever placed on her head.

Much of what had been written about Charest was complimentary in nature, noting his fluency in English and French and his ability to capture votes in Quebec.

In marked contrast to coverage given to Campbell in The Spectator and other media, a Charest visit with delegates in Hamilton prompted the May 25, 1993 Spectator headline: 'Charest rides in on wave,' and an accompanying article, which played up the recent polls along with Charest's assertion that "If we win in Quebec, it's the difference between being the government and being the opposition." 35.

The following day, The Spectator carried a story originating in The Edmonton Journal which suggested Campbell bore many similarities to John Turner – both blue-eyed west coasters had been held out as potential saviours of a troubled party – and wondered if she was about to repeat his experience of a quick rise followed by quick fall from power.

Of course, as it turned out, that's exactly what did happen.

Political history reminds us that Campbell won the party leadership – and became prime minister as a result – only to suffer a humiliating defeat during a federal election that returned the Liberals to power a few months later. 36.

The same day the news article ran, The Spectator carried a column by Don McGillivray who made the identical argument and concluded that:

"Campbell is already embattled to the extent that her ability to win the leadership is in doubt. Between now and June 13, the Tory party establishment will have to decide whether to stick to Ms Campbell or switch support to a largely untested Charest."   37.

These cited observations can be added to the wealth of sources also cited in this chapter, from journalists to political scientists, pollsters and other such political observers who have lent their weight to our central argument that the media and polls can play a highly influential role in elevating candidates and tearing them down, setting the political agenda and determining what issues take the forefront.

We've explored how the media and polls have exercised their influence in the past and we've examined how this again happened in Kim Campbell's briefly successful Tory leadership race, and subsequent devastation at the hands of the electorate.

From all this, we've seen how Campbell initially gained from media exposure and early polling results, then found herself in a defensive and problematic position as the media fell into its time-honoured role of critically scrutinizing the front-runner.

Opinions began to shift and polls soon favoured her rival, Charest.

Certainly, the media influence in agenda-setting and exposing the weaknesses of the leading candidate has succeeded in revealing some troublesome flaws in Campbell: Her ill-advised remarks on the Catholic religion and the disclosure that her ability to speak French is less proficient than she had let on certainly cost her votes from Quebec delegates.

The closeness of the leadership contest certainly indicated that delegates took very seriously Charest's assertions that he could win in Quebec and subsequently form a government.

This winability question, more than Campbell's other embarrassing gaffes over marijuana smoking and an array of seemingly-arrogant statements, came back to haunt her.

Many delegates were convinced that Charest appeared to be more capable of winning in Quebec.

They were also aware of how important a Quebec win would be to the party, to national unity, and to the prospect of being able to add on to such a win by capturing enough additional seats to form a government.

And the delegates were also aware that Charest, unlike Campbell, was a fluently bilingual candidate who had done little to offend significant linguistic or religious groups or embarrass the party.

For all of the above-stated reasons, a good deal of the undecided vote and some of Campbell's 'soft' committed vote did indeed go to Charest on the first ballot, leaving Campbell in a weaker leading position than the overly optimistic delegate support statistics had predicted.

In a scenario somewhat similar – though milder – to that experienced by Flora MacDonald in the 1976 Tory leadership race, Campbell found her first ballot support was weaker than she anticipated.

In contrast, by doing better than expected on the first ballot, Charest initially benefited from a perceived sense of momentum.

Unfortunately for Charest, he was unable to t maintain or add to this momentum and it eventually fizzled out.

Campbell ended up winning the Tory leadership race and became, as a result, prime minister for a just few months, until, that is, the electorate had their say and reduced her to a brief footnote in Canadian political history.

Although Campbell did win the Tory leadership race, there can be little question that the media and polls have again played an influential – if not decisive – role in this race as they have in so many others.

The media's bigger influence may well have been reflected in the electorate's trouncing of

Campbell and the Tories in the federal election.

And although the media has no direct role and, in my view, relatively little influence in shaping government policies, or determining the day-to-day functioning of government, it's clear the media can make a substantial difference when politicians go before delegates or the electorate.

In this 'contest arena' politicians are put under the microscope at a time when their political success or failure is immediately on the line.

At such relatively rare yet critical times, the media can, and often does, play a more central role than usual – if only briefly.

When it comes to critically assessing the leading candidate, raising issues and helping set the political agenda, the messengers – the media and the polls – do indeed play key roles in shaping a leadership race or election.

Chapter Three:
END NOTES:

1. Anthony Wilson-Smith, 'Why Is This Woman Smiling?' Mclean's magazine, March 22, 1993, p. 12. Data and analysis based on poll conducted by Ottawa-based COMPAS Inc., March 1-4, 1993.

2. IBID.

3. IBID, pp. 14-15.

4. IBID, p.13.

5. IBID, p. 14.

6. Anthony Wilson-Smith, 'In Mulroney's Grip,' Mclean's, March 29, 1993, p. 11.

7. Roger Gibbons, Conflict & Unity, (Scarborough: Nelson Canada, '90) p306.

8. As quoted in Mclean's, March 22, 1993, p. 14. Commentary is based on poll conducted for Mclean's by Ottawa-based COMPAS Inc., from March 1-4, 1993.

9. E. Kaye Fulton and Mary Janigan, 'The Real Kim Campbell,' Mclean's. May 17, 1993, p. 16.

10. 'Wilson announces Campbell support for PC leadership' from Canadian Press. as published in The Hamilton Spectator. Tuesday, May 11, 1993, p. A9.

11. IBID.

12. 'Campbell is overconfident Charest claims,' from Canadian Press, as published in The Hamilton Spectator. Tuesday, May 18, 1993, p. A7.

13. 'Campbell sorry – 'Enemies' too strong a word,' CP, The Hamilton Spectator, Saturday, May 15, 1993, p. A6.

14. Ross Howard, 'Campbell style target of ploy by Charest camp – Potentially incendiary phrases brought to attention of reporters,' The Globe and Mail, May 19, 1993, p. A1.

15. John Geddes, 'Campbell comments defended,' The Financial Post May 19, 1993, p. 5.

16. Toronto Star staff and CP 'No need to apologize: Campbell,' The Toronto Star, May 19, 1993, p. A11.

17. Carol Goar, 'Campbell displays resilience in last Tory debate,' The Toronto Star, May 19, 1993, pp. Al and A24.

18. Peter O'Neil, 'It's a good thing that we're getting to know Kim Campbell,' The Vancouver Sun, May 21, 1993, p. A10.

19. IBID.

20. Canadian Press, 'Poll shows Charest to win Quebec in election,' as published in The Spectator, May 21, 1993. p. A7.

21. Canadian Press. 'Charest overtakes Campbell in latest public opinion polls,' The Spectator May 25, 1993. p. Al0.

22. Marc Clark and Lisa Van Dusen, Strength in the Heartland, from Canadian Politics 91/92, (Guilford, Connecticut: Dushkin Publishing Group, 1991), p. 107.

23. John Flanders, 'The undecided are really undecided,' Spectator, May 22, '93, p A8.

24. Jeffrey Simpson, 'Pollstruck,' from Crosscurrents. Contemporary Political Issues, edited by Mark Chariton and Paul Barker, (Scarborough: Nelson Canada, 1991), p. 299.

25. Canadian Press, 'Campbell gives her side of the story to delegates,' from The Hamilton Spectator. May 28, 1993, p. A3. Also: CP, 'Campbell on defensive says 'I believe in truth,' from The Hamilton Spectator, May 19, 1993, p. A3.

26. Jeffrey Simpson, 'Pollstruck' from Crosscurrents. Contemporary Political Issues, edited by Mark Chariton and Paul Barker, (Scarborough: Nelson Canada, 1991), p. 298.

27. Clive Cocking, Following the Leaders: A Media Watcher's Diary of Campaign '79 (Toronto: Doubleday, 1980), p. 111.

28. Mark 0. Dickerson, Thomas Flanagan & Neil Nevitte, Introductory Readings in Government and Politics, (Scarborough: Nelson Canada, 1988), p. 273.

29. Christina McCall-Newman, Grits. An Intimate Portrait oft he Liberal Party, (Toronto: Macmillan Canada 1982)p.108.

30. Frederick J. Fletcher and Daphne Gottlieb Taras, 'Images and Issues: The Mass Media and Politics in Canada' from Canadian Politics in the 1990s, Third Edition, edited by Michael S. Whittington and Glen Williams, (Scarborough: Nelson Canada, 1990), p. 238.

31. Mark 0. Dickerson and Thomas Flanagan, An Introduction to Government & Politics, (Scarborough: Nelson Canada, 1990), p. 300.

32. Robert A. Hackett and Lynne Hissey, 'Who Sets the Agenda? Perspectives on Media and Party Politics in Canada, from Party Politics in Canada, 6th Edition, edited by Hugh G. Thorburn, (Scarborough: Prentice-Hall Canada, 1991), pp. 42-43.

33. CBC Newsworld Television Network coverage of Campbell marijuana-smoking issue, May 20, 1993.

34. Canadian Press 'Campbell sorry she told truth about pot,' The Hamilton Spectator, May 22, 1993, p. A4.

35. Caroline Nolan, 'Charest rides in on wave,' The Hamilton Spectator May 25, 1993, p. B3.

36. Norm Ovenden, 'Will Kim Campbell repeat John Turner's fate?' The Hamilton Spectator, May 26, 1993, p. All.

37. Don McGillivray, 'Campbell is already embattled and the Tories are losing the war,' The Hamilton Spectator, May 26, 1993, p. A6.

BIBLIOGRAPHY

Act of Faith: The illustrated chronicle of the Reform Party of Canada. Vancouver: B.C. Report Magazine Ltd., 1991.

Adams, Chris, 'The Reform Party and the Roots of Western Protest', Parliamentary Government. Vol.9. No. 1. Ottawa: Fall, 1989.

Annual Editions: Canadian Politics. 91192. Guilford, Connecticut: Dushkin Publishing Group Inc., 1991.

Bashevkin, Sylvia, Toeing the Lines: Women and Party Politics in English Canada. Toronto: University of Toronto Press, 1985.

Brodie, Janine and Vickers, Jill McCalla, 'Canadian Women in Politics: An Overview,' The Politics of the Second Electorate, Ottawa, 1982.

Brodie, Janine, The Gender Factor and National Leadership Conventions in Canada," Party Democracy in Canada, Toronto: Prentice Hall, 1988.

Brodie, Janine. 'Women and the Electoral Process in Canada,' Women in Canadian Politics: Toward Equity in Representation. Toronto: Dundurn Press, 1992.

Burt, Sandra, "Women's issues and the Women's Movement in Canada since 1970," The Politics of Gender, Ethnicity and Language in Canada. Edited by Alan Cairns and Cynthia Williams, Toronto: University of Toronto Press, 1986.

Canadian Press, 'Campbell gives her side of the story to delegates,' The Hamilton Spectator, May 28, 1993.

Canadian Press, 'Campbell on defensive says 'I believe in truth,' The Hamilton Spectator, May 19, 1993.

Canadian Press, 'Campbell sorry - 'Enemies' too strong a word,' The Hamilton Spectator, May 15, 1993.

Canadian Press, 'Campbell sorry she told truth about pot,' The Hamilton Spectator, May 22, 1993.

Canadian Press, 'Charest overtakes Campbell in latest public opinion polls,' The Hamilton Spectator, May 25, 1993.

Canadian Press, 'Poll shows Charest to win Quebec in election,' The Hamilton Spectator, May 21, 1993.

Canadian Press, 'Wilson announces Campbell support for PC leadership,' The Hamilton Spectator, May 11, 1993.

Canadian. Press, 'Campbell is overconfident, Charest claims,' The Hamilton Spectator, May 18, 1993.

CBC Newsworld Television Network coverage of Campbell marijuana-smoking issue, May 20, 1993.

Cocking, Clive, Following the Leaders: A Media Watcher's Diary of Campaign '79, Toronto: Doubleday, 1980.

Coote, Anna and Pattullo, Polly. Power and Prejudice. Women and Politics. London: Weidenfeld and Nicholson, 1990.

Dickerson, Mark, 0. and Flanagan, Thomas, An Introduction to Government & Politics, Scarborough: Nelson Canada, 1990.

Dickerson, Mark, 0. Flanagan, Thomas & Nevitte, Neil, Introductory Readings in Government and Politics, Scarborough: Nelson Canada, 1988.

Dobbin, Murray, Preston Manning and the Reform Party. Toronto: James Lorimer & Company, Publishers, 1991.

Duverger, Maurice, The Political Role of Women, United Nations Commission on the Status of Women/ Unesco, Paris, 1953.

Faure, Christine, Democracy Without Women, Indianapolis, Ind.: Indiana University Press, 1985.

Finkle, Alvin, The Social Credit Phenomenon in Alberta. Toronto: University of Toronto Press, 1989.

Flanders, John, 'The undecided are really undecided,' The Hamilton Spectator, May 22, 1993.

Fletcher, Frederick, J. and Taras, Daphne, Gottlieb, 'Images and Issues: The Mass Media and Politics in Canada, Canadian Politics in the 1990s, Third Edition, edited by Michael S. Whittington and Glen Williams, Scarborough: Nelson Canada, 1990.

Fulton, E. Kaye, and Janigan, Mary, 'The Real Kim Campbell,' Mclean's, May 17, 1993.

Geddes, John, 'Campbell comments defended,' The Financial Post, May 19, 1993.

Gibbons, Roger, Conflict & Unity, Scarborough: Nelson Canada, 1990.

Githens, Marianne, Political Women. Edited by Janet A. Flammang, London: Sage Publications Inc., 1984.

Goar, Carol, 'Campbell displays resilience in last Tory debate,' The Toronto Star, May 19, 1993.

Gotell, Lise and Brodie, Janine. 'Women and Politics: More than an Issue of Numbers,' Party Politics in Canada, edited by Hugh G. Thorburn. Scarborough: Prentice-Hall of Canada, 1991.

Hackett, Robert, A. and Hissey, Lynne, 'Who Sets the Agenda? Perspectives on Media and Politics in Canada, Party Politics in Canada, 6th Edition, edited by Hugh G. Thorburn, Scarborough: Prentice-Hall Canada, 1991.

Hebert, Chantal, 'Chretien marching to Alliance drummer', The Toronto Star, October 31, 2001.

Howard, Ross, 'Campbell style target of ploy by Charest camp – Potentially incendiary phrases brought to attention of reporters,' The Globe and Mail, May 19, 1993.

Irving, John, A. The Social Credit Movement in Alberta. Toronto: University of Toronto Press, 1974.

Keal V, Linda and Sangster, Joan. Beyond the Vote. Canadian Women and Politics, Toronto: University of Toronto Press, 1989.

Kohn, Walter S. G., "Women in the Canadian House of Commons," American Review of Canadian Studies, Vol. 3, 1984.

MacGregor, Roy, 'Preston Manning goes to Ottawa and talks common sense', The Hamilton Spectator. October 4, 1991.

MacPherson, C. B. Democracy in Alberta: Social Credit and the Party System. Toronto: University of Toronto Press, 1962.

Maille, Chantal. 'Primed for Power: Women in Canadian Politics,' Background Paper for Canadian Advisory Council on Status of Women, November 1990.

Manning, Preston, The New Canada. Toronto: Macmillan Canada, 1992.

Matlin, Margaret W. The Psychology of Women, Toronto: Holt, Rinehart and Winston Inc., 1987.

McCall-Newman, Christina, Gras. An Intimate Portrait of the Liberal Party, Toronto: Macmillan of Canada, 1982.

McCormick, Peter, 'The Reform Party of Canada: New Beginning or Dead End?', Party Politics in Canada. edited by Hugh G. Thorburn, Scarborough: Prentice-Hall Canada, 1991.

McGillivray, Don, 'Campbell is already embattled and the Tories are losing the war,' The Hamilton Spectator, May 26, 1993.

Mclean's, March 22, 1993.

Morgan, Nicole. The Equality Game. Women in the Federal Public Service (1908-1987). Ottawa: Canadian Advisory Council on the Status of Women, 1988.

Nolan, Caroline, 'Charest rides in on wave,' The Hamilton Spectator, May 25, 1993.

O'Neil, Peter, 'It's a good thing that we're getting to know Kim Campbell,' The Vancouver Sun, Friday, May 21, 1993.

Ovendun, Norm, 'Will Kim Campbell repeat John Turner's fate?' The Hamilton Spectator, May 26, 1993.

Poole, Keith T. and Zeigler, Harmon L. Women, Pubic Opinion, and Politics. New York: Longman Inc., 1985.

Principles and Policies: The Blue Book 1991. Calgary: Reform Fund Canada, 1991.

Sharpe, Sydney, and Braid, Don, Storming Babylon. Preston Manning and the Rise of the Reform Party. Toronto: Key Porter Books, 1992.

Simpson, Jeffrey, 'Pollstruck,' Crosscurrents. Contemporary Political Issues, edited by Mark Chariton and Paul Barker, Scarborough: Nelson Canada, 1991.

Status of Women Canada, Federal Government of Canada, Towards Equality For Women. Minister of Supply and Services Canada, 1979.

Thorburn, Hugh, G. Party Politics in Canada. edited by Hugh G. Thorburn, Scarborough: Prentice-Hall Canada, 1991.

Toronto Star staff , CP 'No need to apologize: Campbell,' The Toronto Star, May 19, 1993.

Trickey, Mike, 'Manning tells students beware of unity deal', The Hamilton Spectator. September 29, 1992.

Whyte, Kenneth, with co-writers, 'The West Finds a Voice: A new federal party is launched', Act of Faith: The Illustrated Chronicle of the Reform Party of Canada. Vancouver: B.C. Report Magazine, 1991.

Wilson-Smith, Anthony, 'In Mulroney's Grip,' Mclean's March 29, 1993.

Wilson-Smith, Anthony, 'Why Is This Woman Smiling?' Mclean's magazine, March 22, 1993.

Manor House Publishing Inc.
(905) 648-2193